I'M 50 Sassy AND ALL KINDS OF Classy

Keep Calm
AND BE
FABULOUS
AT 50

DO YOU KNOW
THE AGE OF
MOST SEXY
WOMEN?
50
Of Course

HAPPY
Birthday
TO YOU

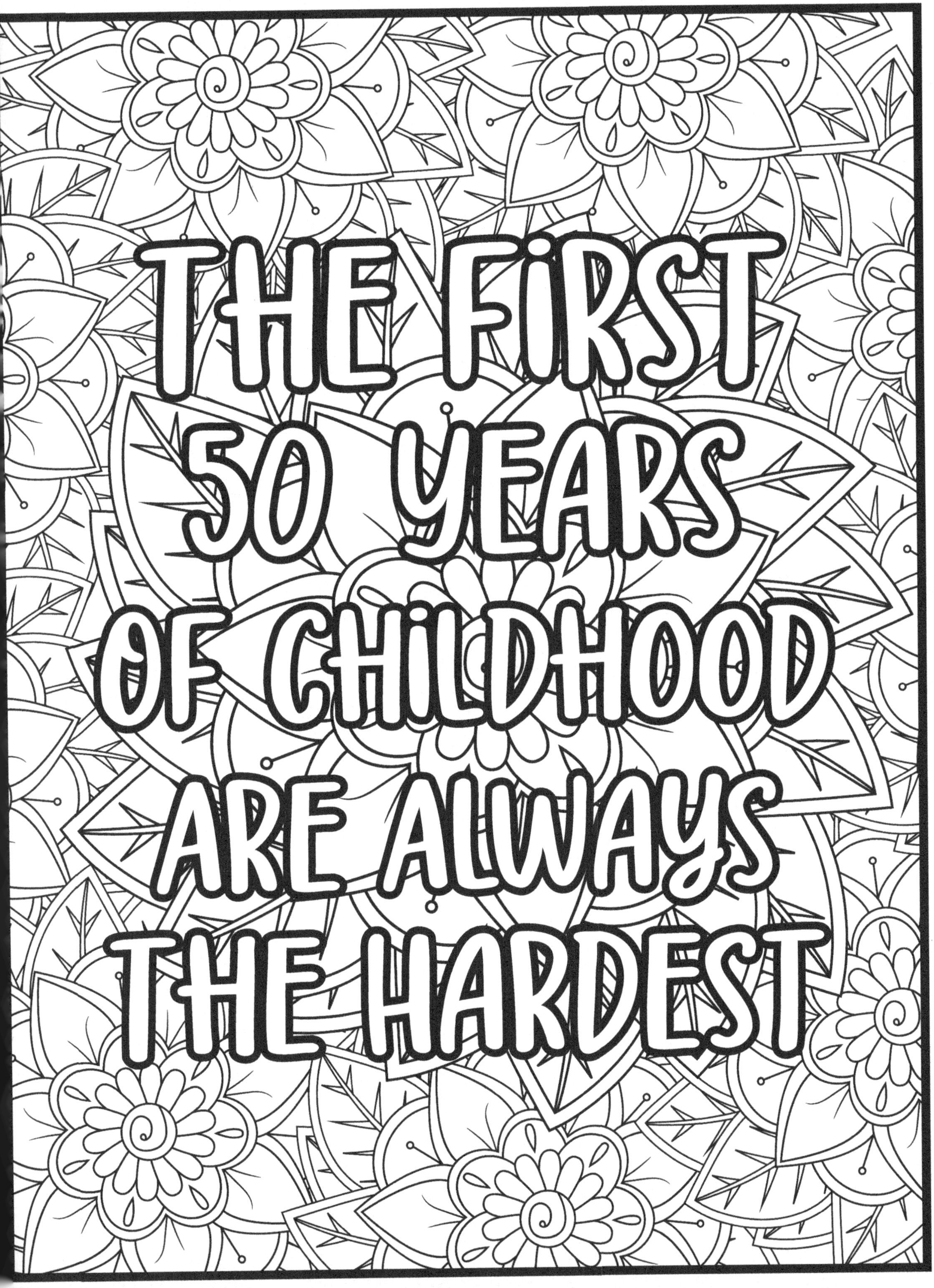
THE FIRST
50 YEARS
OF CHILDHOOD
ARE ALWAYS
THE HARDEST

Cheers
to 50
Years

ENHALE
CouraGe
EXHALE
Fear

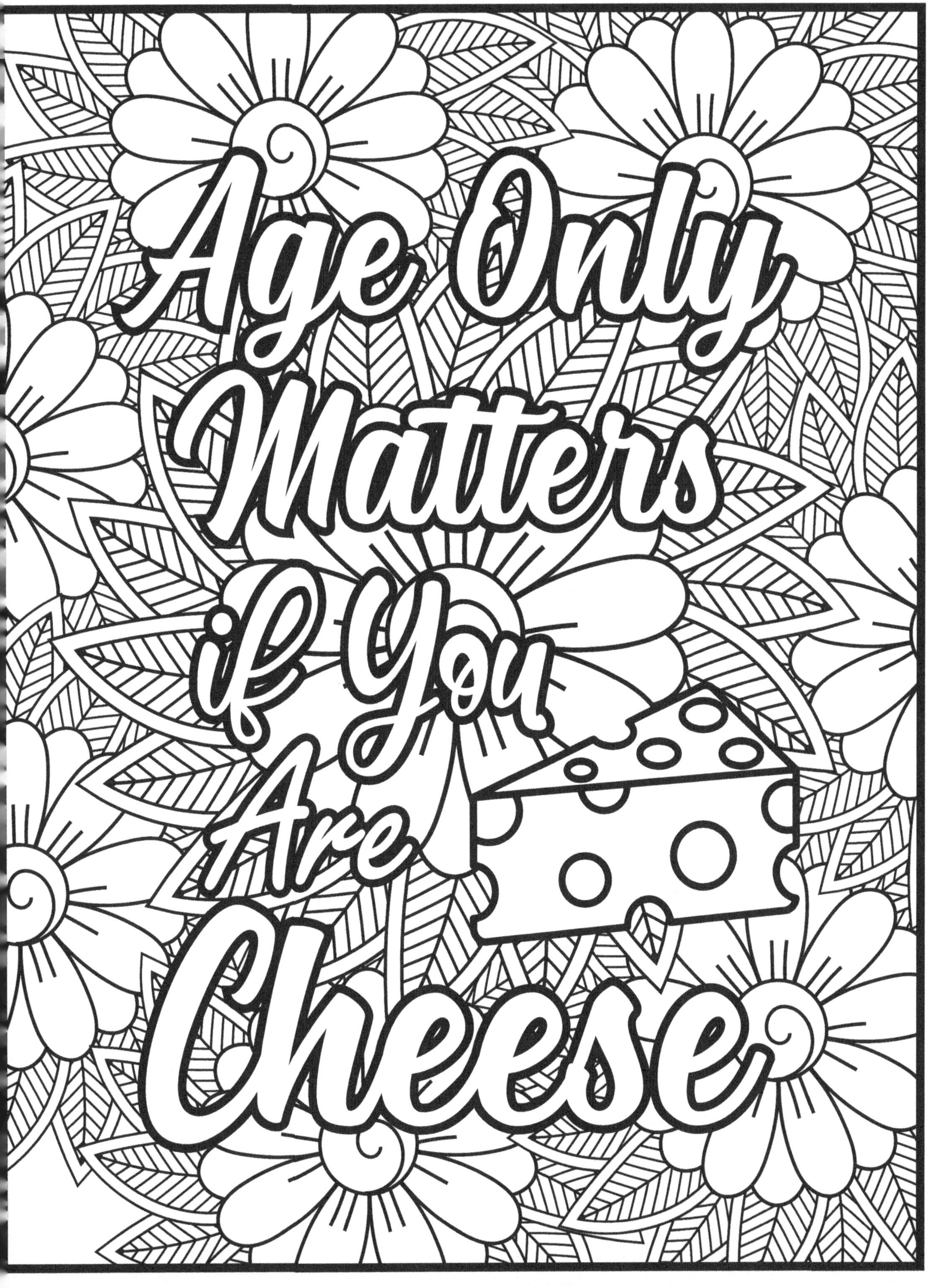
Age Only
Matters
if You
Are
Cheese

BLOW ME
I'M 50

opportunities
Are All
AROUND
ME

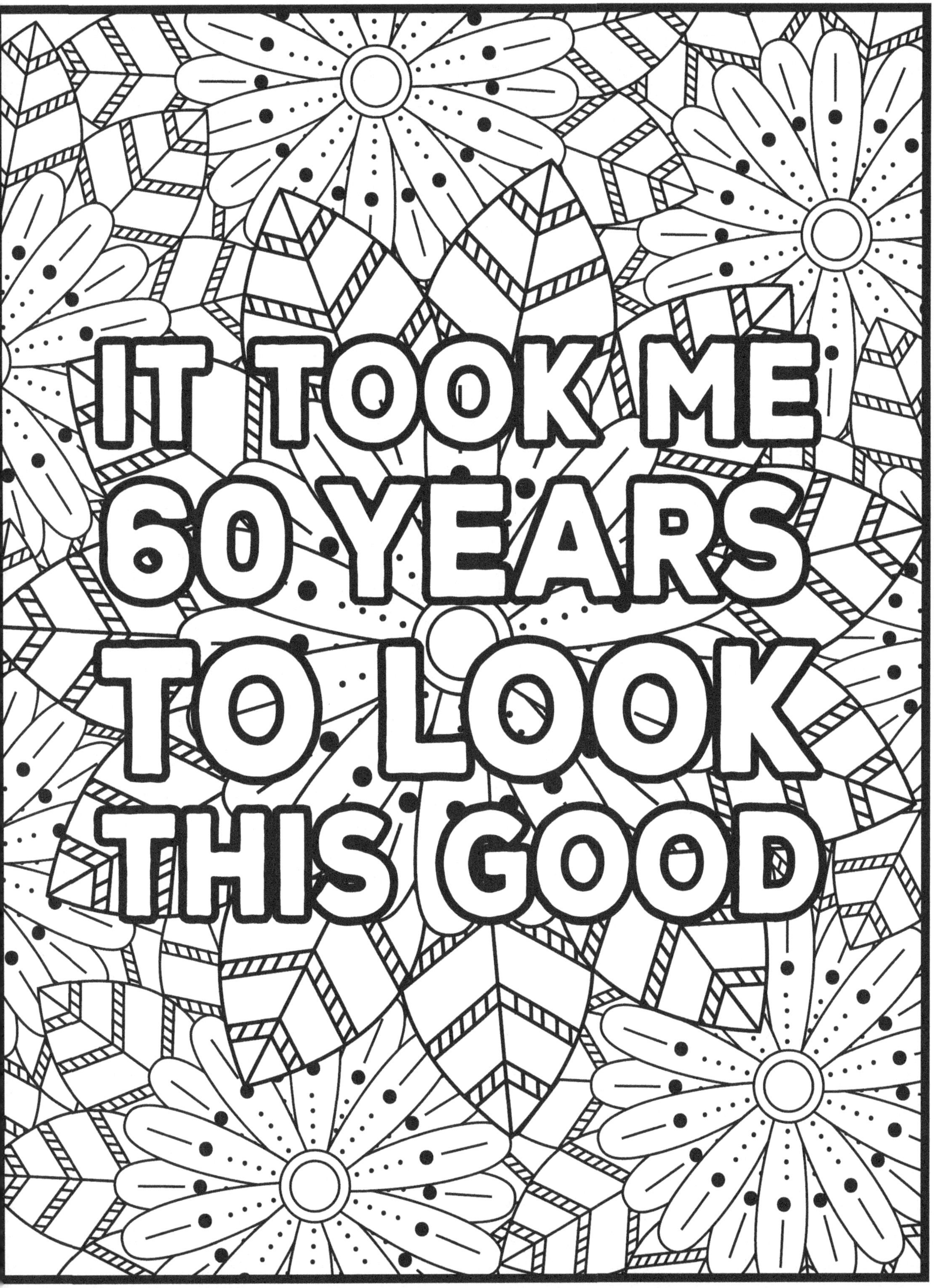
IT TOOK ME
60 YEARS
TO LOOK
THIS GOOD

IMPOSSIBLE
Is Just An
OPINION

AGING IS THE
WORST SIDE
EFFECT OF
BIRTHDAYS

Great
News
You're still
Alive

I'm
49+

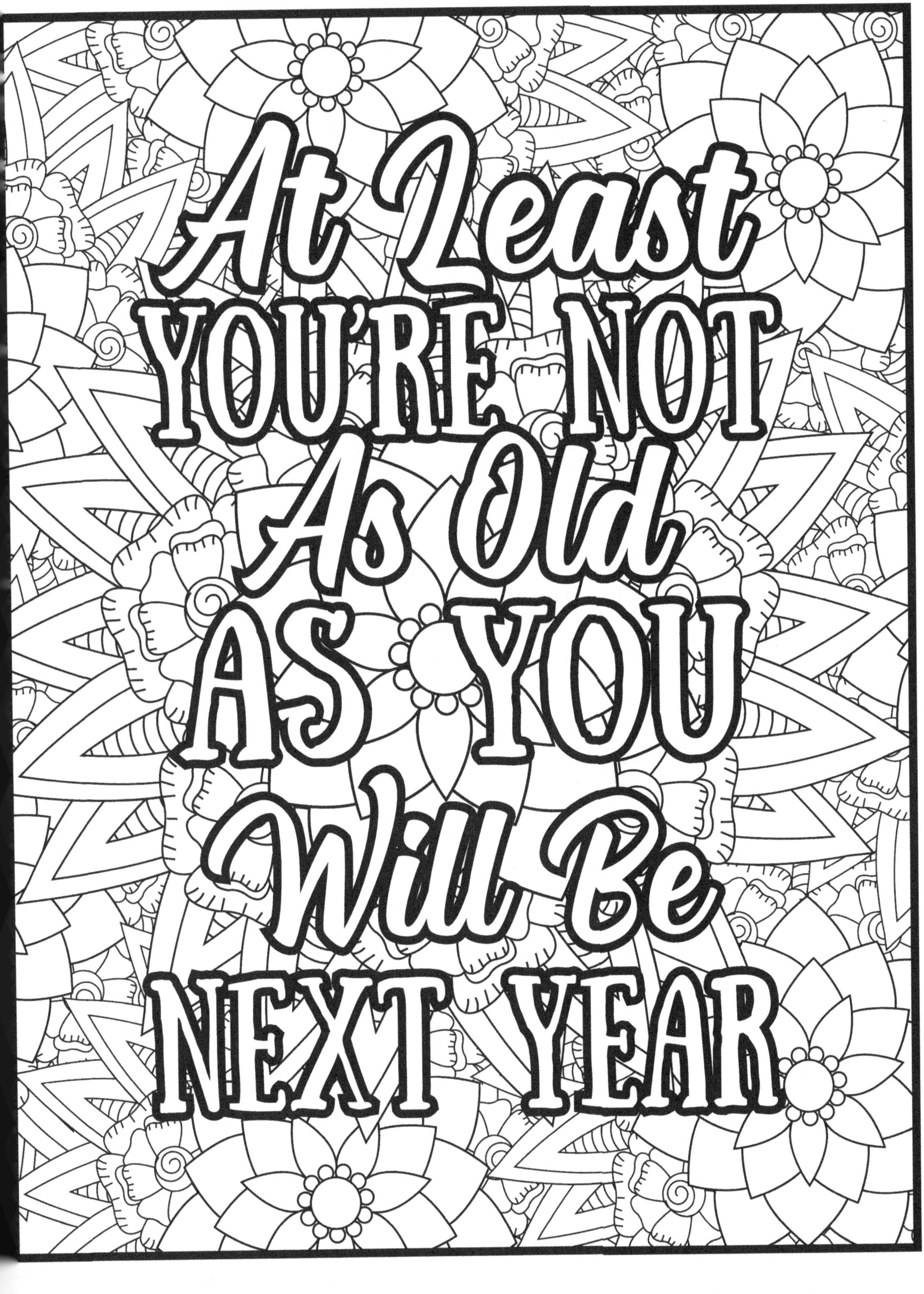
At Least
YOU'RE NOT
As Old
AS YOU
Will Be
NEXT YEAR

TURNING
50 LIKE:
I CAN FEEL
MYSELF
ROTTING.

BELIVE IN
Your Own
CREATIVE
POWER

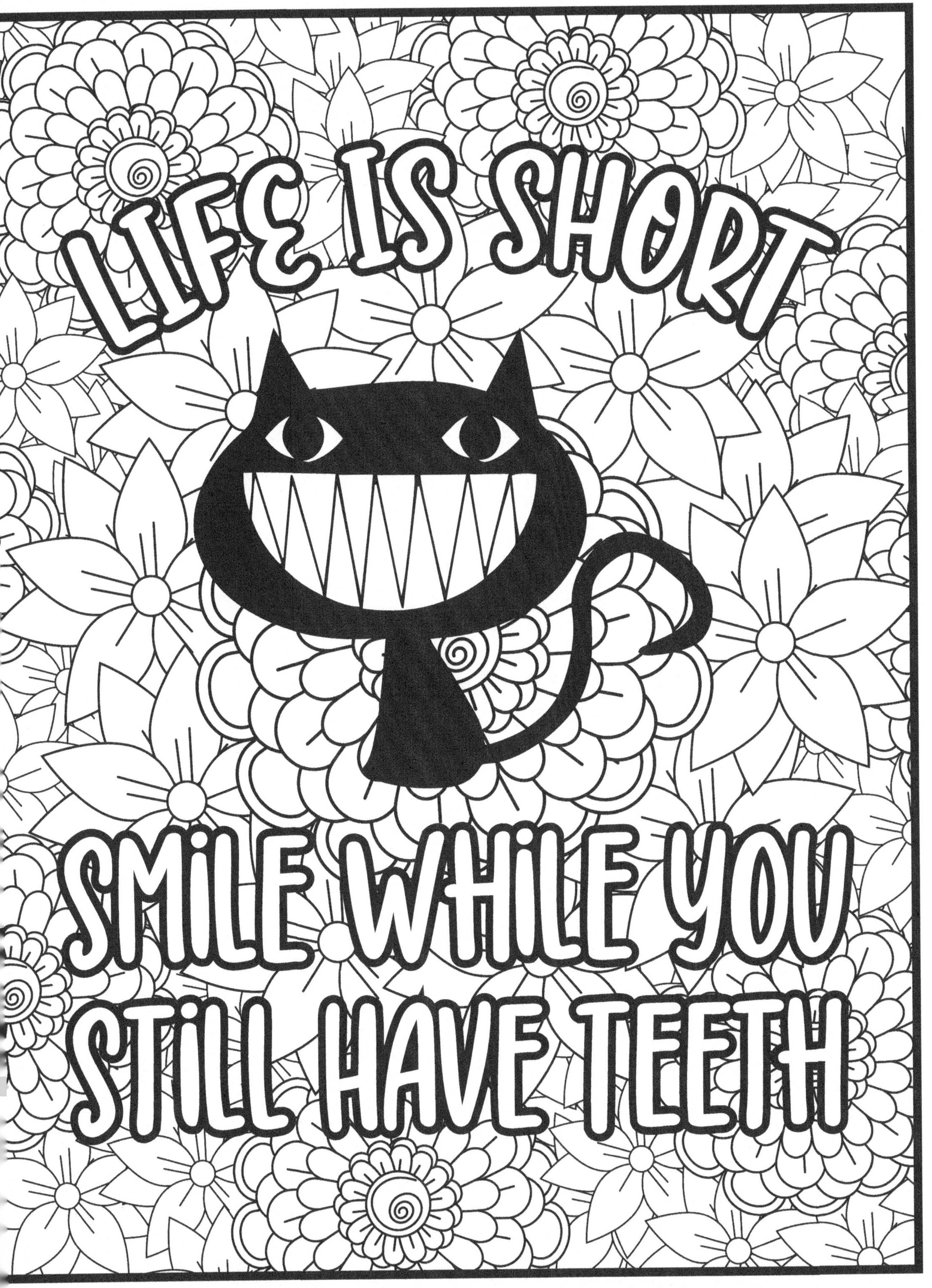
LIFE IS SHORT
SMILE WHILE YOU
STILL HAVE TEETH

You Are too
HANDSOME
At the age of
50

LET YOUR
HEART
Speak

Now
or
Never

Damn
I MAKE
50
LOOKS GOOD

Keep Life simple

You Are
Made Of
MAGIC

Everyday
Is A Fresh
Start

Focus
on the
Good

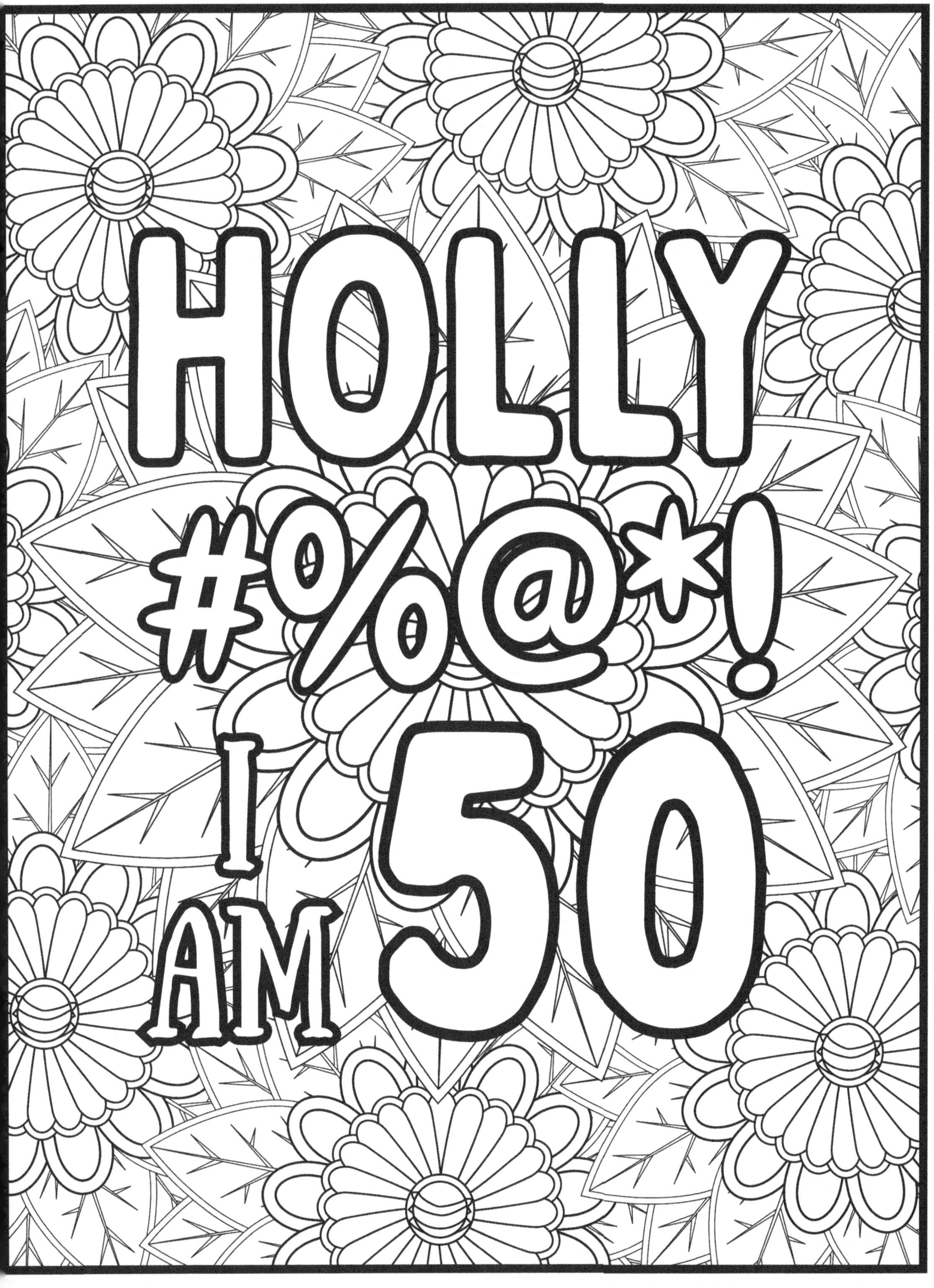
HOLLY
#%@*!
I AM 50

50
& AGED TO
Perfection

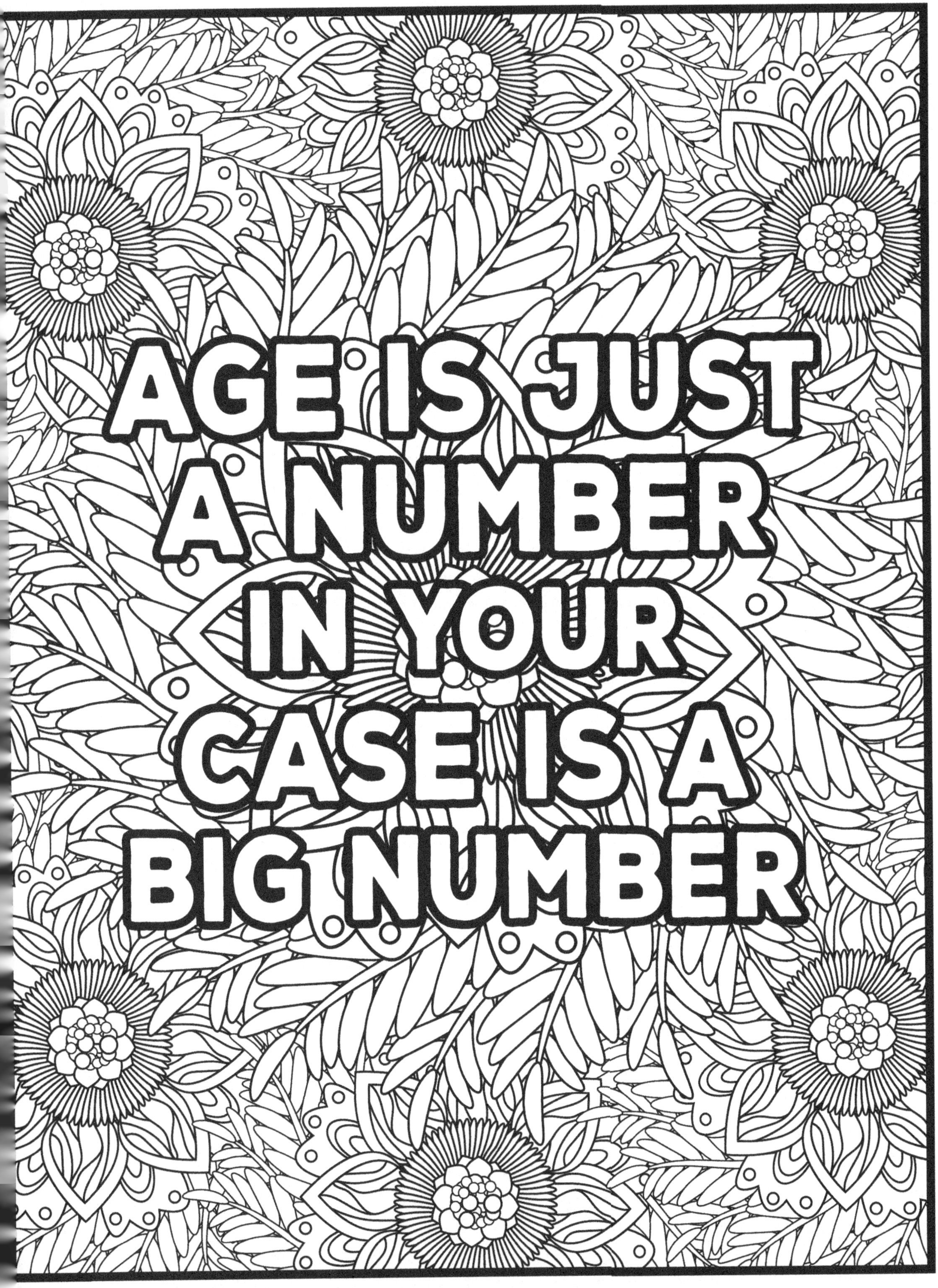
AGE IS JUST
A NUMBER
IN YOUR
CASE IS A
BIG NUMBER

Hey, You're So GREAT

CONGRATS
FOR BEING
BORN MANY
YEARS AGO

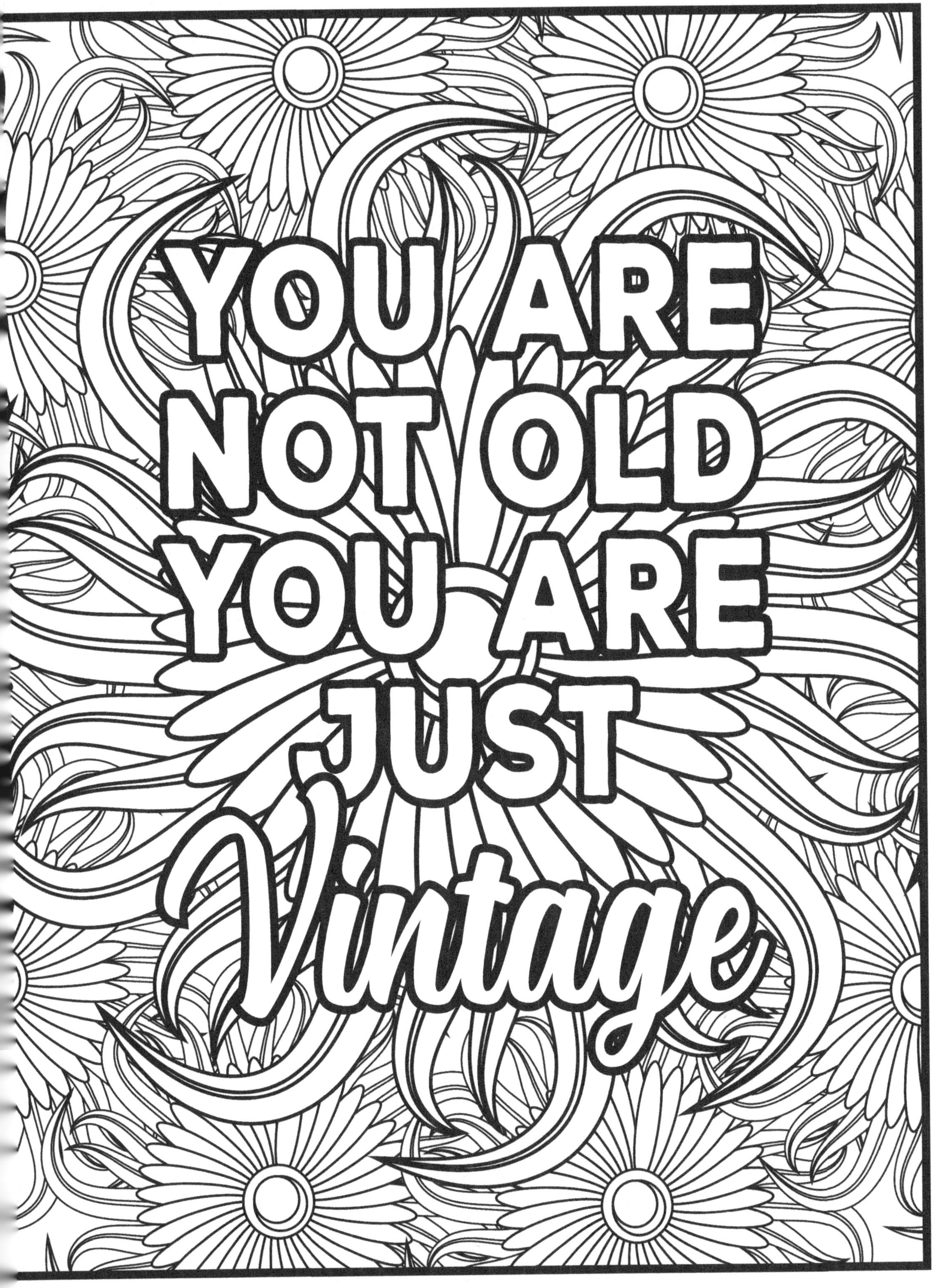
YOU ARE
NOT OLD
YOU ARE
JUST
Vintage

Be the Light
You're amazing

SO!
I DEMAND
A RECOUNT

Be
Strong
BELIEVE
in
YOURSELF

CLEAN
Your Mind
ENJOY
Every Moment

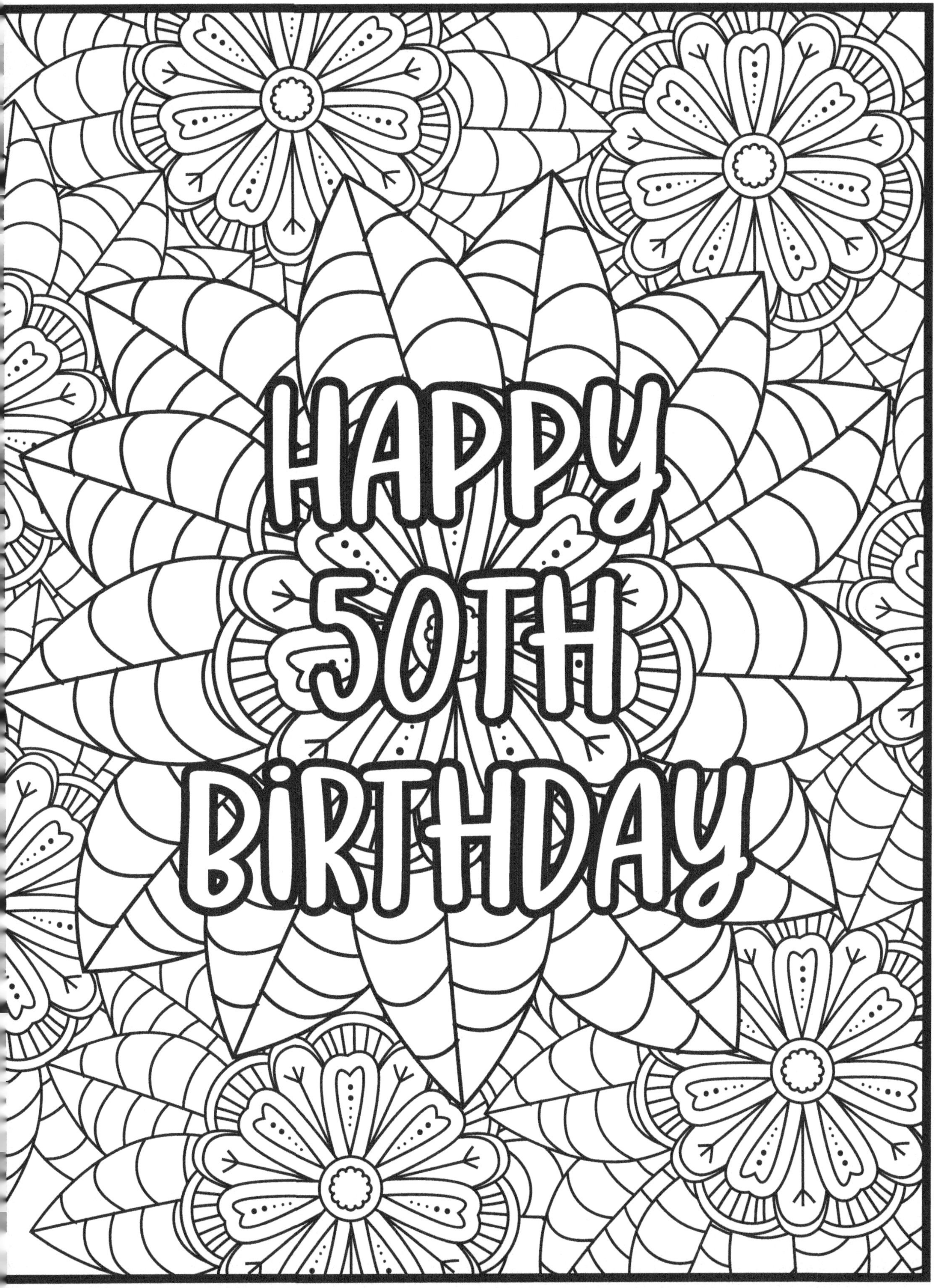
HAPPY
50TH
BIRTHDAY

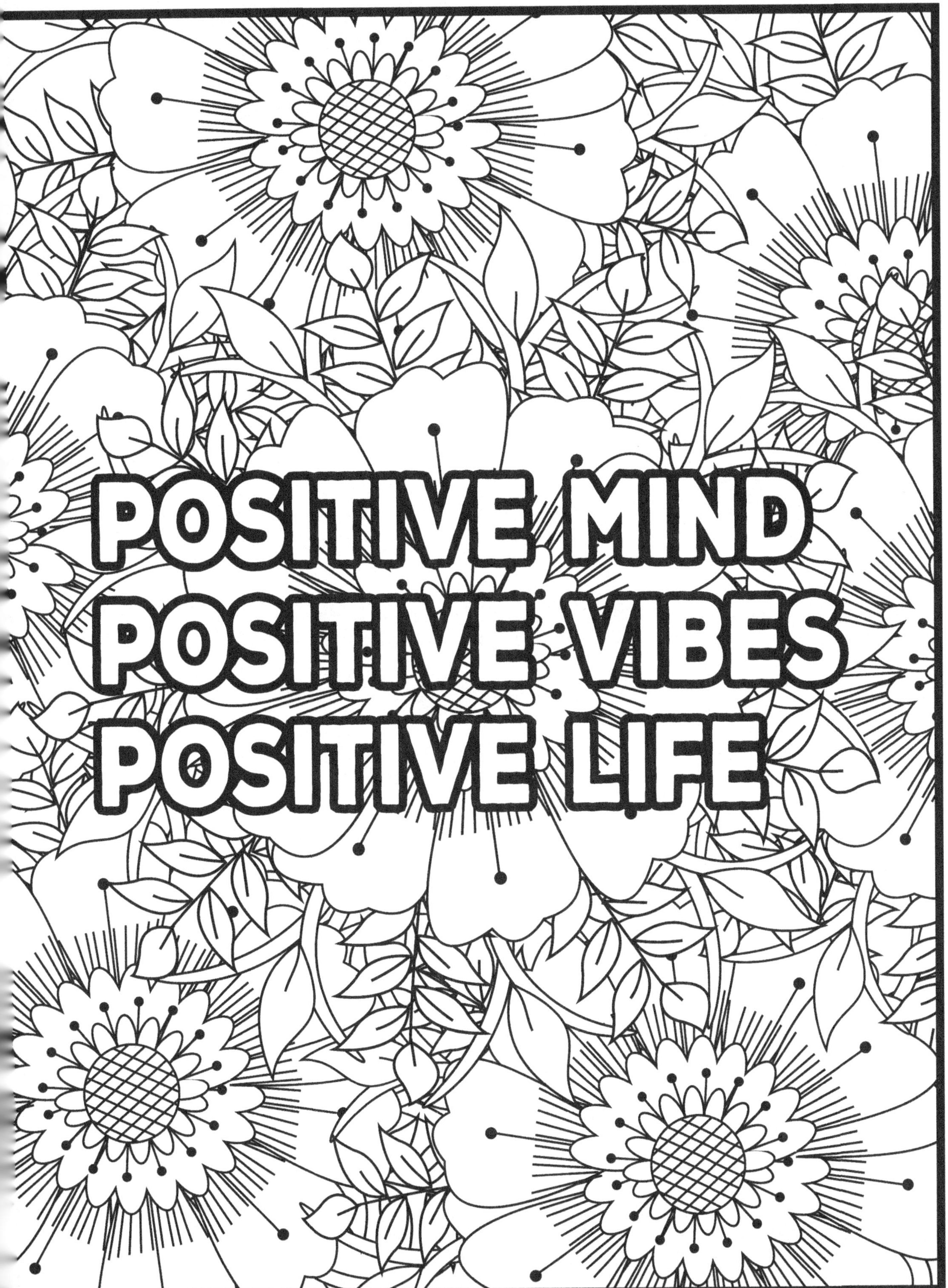
POSITIVE MIND
POSITIVE VIBES
POSITIVE LIFE

Test Your Colors

☆☆☆☆☆

Don't forget to
give us your opinion
By leaving a review

Made in the USA
Columbia, SC
21 November 2024

47208424R00046